Abraham 101

The basics of the Law of Attraction as taught by Abraham and Understood by Me

Zehra Mahoon

"Everyone is creating, because everyone is thinking."

~ Abraham

Abraham 101

The basics of the Law of Attraction
as taught by Abraham and
Understood by Me

Zehra Mahoon

Table of Contents

"If you will let your standard of success be your achievement of joy – everything else will fall easily into place."
~ Abraham

Why I wrote this book

I stand witness to the evolution of Abraham's message over the years. The message has not changed – it has evolved in its clarity and specificity. Abraham continues to find analogies that will depict the concept of the Law of Attraction. The varied ways in which Abraham offer their teachings is meant to resonate with a varied set of people, therefore increasing the circumference of those who are able to grasp and understand the message.

Sometime ago Steve emailed me expressing confusion in understanding the terms and analogies that Abraham has used over the years and how they are connected. As a result this little book was inspired.

Over the years, Abraham has created a terminology that they use to explain the law of attraction. Every time they start using a new phrase they take the time to explain it in detail. When they sense that people in the audience are not familiar with a certain terminology they explain it again. But when we listen to Abraham material on YouTube, or purchase audio programs, the original sequence of things is lost and the explanation of terms and phrases and analogies is lost.

Abraham offers two types of analogies. The first type is a broad analogy that is like the foundation stone of the teachings. This type of analogy includes the concept of the stream, the vortex, the grid and the emotional scale and swirling discs and more recently the hills of San Francisco. The second type of analogy is used in transition to explain a situation or event or to add clarity to the answer given in response to a question coming from the "**hot seat**"[1]. The second type of analogy adds additional clarity to the first broad based type but is not a consistent part of the terminology that has over the years become Abraham specific. In this book, I am including the first, broad type analogy and will use a limited number of the second type.

Abraham also teaches **Processes**[2]. Processes are actions we can take to create **ease and flow**[3] in

---

[1] Hot seat is the chair placed on the stage in all Abraham workshops, to which members of the audience are invited to sit in and ask their questions, and receive Abraham's response.

[2] Processes are given in the book Ask & It is Given. Processes include Focus Wheels, Meditation, and Pre-paving, but there are

our lives. Processes help in reducing **Resistance**[4] and bring us into **Alignment**[5]. Being in a state of alignment is conducive to the **Manifestation**[6] of all things that we want in our physical reality.

To be completely honest, this is my interpretation of the teachings of Abraham, written in an effort to help others like myself who want to accelerate their personal learning and growth. Some of you might have your own interpretation of Abraham's teachings, and that's Ok too. We each take what we need and make it our own. This is not an official rendering of

---

also specific processes for creating abundance and other things enumerated in the book.

[3] "Ease and Flow" is a phrase used often by Abraham. It is a feeling. It is the feeling of being able to achieve everything easily in life. Being relaxed.

[4] Resistance is the opposite of ease and flow. It is a feeling of not being able to achieve everything easily in life. At its peak, resistance is a feeling of worry, anxiety and anger. At the lowest level, resistance is the feeling of not liking something or thinking that something is hard or impossible.

[5] Alignment is a feeling of Love or a feeling of Joy. Abraham says that when we are in alignment, we see things through the eyes of Source.

[6] Manifestation is a state of physical reality – it occurs when we can smell, taste, see, hear, touch the object of our desire.

Abraham's teachings offered by Abraham-Hicks Publication.

I hope you find this dissertation useful and I hope it helps you on your way.

Much love and appreciation,

Zehra

"Feel your way forward."
~ Abraham

Esther & Jerry Hicks

Esther & Jerry Hicks began a new journey in 1985 when Esther started receiving Abraham.

The best place to read up on the details of how it all started is to go to the Abraham-Hicks official website. I also found the DVD "The secret behind the secret" extremely helpful in understanding why Esther and Jerry devoted their lives to spreading the teachings of Abraham.

From my personal perspective, there were a few things that stood out, here they are briefly explained:

1. Jerry had always been asking questions about why life treated certain people one way and other people another. He had changed his life in many ways, he had changed his health, his prosperity and his relationships, and he wanted to find a way that would work every time that he could teach others to improve their lives.

2. Esther was always a carefree and happy person. Esther was Jerry's secretary before they got married in 1980.

3. Jerry and Esther, had only been married a few years when in 1985 they visited Theo (another non-physical energy) and started meditating on a regular basis until one day Esther recognized that an energy inside her was trying to communicate with her.

4. Jerry and Esther were already financially stable and had the resources to pursue whatever captured their fancy. It was never their intention to use the teachings of Abraham for financial gain, they just wanted to teach and break even on their costs in the process. Jerry was a successful Amway distributor, he also owned and operated motels and had some interests in the entertainment industry.

5. Esther has a daughter, Tracy, and two grandchildren Kate and Luke. Tracy works at Abraham Hicks publication. Her husband runs the company that organizes the Abraham Hicks cruises.

6. Jerry has children from earlier relationships, but I don't know much about them.

7. The very first gatherings took place at Esther and Jerry's home, and later at meeting venues around the USA. Eventually Jerry and Esther bought a "monster bus" and had it custom fitted to serve as their home on the road. Esther always drove.

8. After many years of travelling and offering weekend workshops Jerry and Esther gave up the monster bus in favor of air flight.

9. All the books and other materials published by Abraham-Hicks publications are written by Abraham.

10. Jerry Hicks died of cancer at age 87 in November 2011. Esther was born in 1948. There were 24 years between then two of them.

"A happy life is just a string of happy moments – but most people don't allow the happy moment, because they're so busy trying to get a happy life."
~ Abraham

The Basic Tenants of the Law of Attraction

The Abraham-Hicks official website has a brief introduction to the teachings of Abraham.[7] All books published by Abraham-Hicks Publications also contain a detailed explanation of the law of attraction as taught by Abraham.

For the purposes of this writing, here is a summary:

1. We can have be or do anything we want. And by the same token we can change things in our life at any time. There is no karma or destiny.

2. We create everything that happens in our life by our power to think.

3. Our emotions provide us guidance in what is good for us and what is not.

4. We are part of a collective consciousness.

5. We are always loved by the collective consciousness and always connected to it.

---

[7] Link to the official Abraham-Hicks website http://www.abraham-hicks.com/lawofattractionsource/about_abraham.php

6. The purpose of our life is to experience joy. There is nothing for us to fix and no lessons to be learnt.

7. You never get it done and you cannot get it wrong.

8. Feel good and good things happen.

9. If you make a decision, then line-up with it – make it good.

10. There is no death, just a change of perspective.

11. All is well at all times.

"You don't need to get your mind out of the way, you need to guide it."
~ Abraham

What is Source, Who is God?

Abraham continuously refers to the words "**Source**", and "**Universe**". It is clear that these words are used to replace the word "**God**". The question is why come up with new terminology to refer to God?

Around the world, many different words are used to denote God, based on language and religion. In using the terms "Universe" and "Source", Abraham is stepping away from all of them. Abraham has said on many occasions that they are doing so in order to step away from the incorrect beliefs that man has attached to the interpretation of who God is.

For example, in some faiths and religions there is the concept of the "wrath of God", that if you don't behave in a manner that dogma has prescribed as being proper and right that God will exercise vengeance upon you in this world, and in this life, and in addition, upon death you will go to "hell" forever or until such time as you repent your sins. The same religions also teach us about a God who is all forgiving and loving.

Abraham, steps away from this philosophy by stating that God or Source is all loving. Source never exacts any punishment, and there is no hell except in our own minds. Abraham does say that if we think thoughts or engage in actions that we believe are not right or that feel bad, this results in less than wanted events happening in our lives. This is the law of attraction in action and not an exacting of punishment from the heavens above or the wrath of God.

"You are the leading edge of that which you think God is."
~ Abraham

The word Source when used for God, indicates that we all come from that Source and we all return to Source, and we are connected to Source in every living moment. At any point in time, our connection with Source can be free flowing, and when it is, we experience joy or a free flowing love.

To me, Source is God, and God is Source. Source is where we all come from, and where we all return. Source is like an ocean, that sends out waves in the form of all living things including plants, animals and humans. Each wave runs its course and returns back to the ocean, just like we are born, and have distinct, unique personalities, and unique lives, and then we transition

12

through the death experience returning to Source – and at all times remaining connected to Source. (I learnt this analogy from Deepak Chopra).

This is why Source is a collective. Just like the ocean is made up of drops of water, Source is made up of souls or points of consciousness. Source is connected to us at all times, and so Source can focus through our eyes or the eyes of a fly, or both at the same time. We are all extensions of Source, and when we are aligned we can call information and resources through our connection with Source. Source knows everything, and is everywhere at the same time, omniscient, omnipresent, infinite.

"A creator is one who focuses energy."
~ Abraham

Who is Abraham?

It took me a long time to figure out the answer to this question, but I'm quite happy with my understanding – it makes sense to me. I humbly suggest that you read this section, contemplate it and then return to it after once having completed a reading of this book in its entirety. I promise you that what I say here will make a lot more sense to you once you have completed an initial discovery into the teachings of Abraham.

Please try to look at it this way: Esther Hicks is like a drop of water that can maintain its individual existence (and perspective) and at the same time can at will reach into the ocean that is Source and become one with it, giving her the ability to draw information and answers from it. When she does this she dons the perspective of the ocean and this perspective is what she calls "Abraham". This is why "Abraham" is referred to by her as "they", because Abraham is many individual perspectives or drops of water that can coalesce into one perspective – the all knowing perspective of Source. By doing so the individual drops don't lose their individuality, they always have that, which is why those who transition (or kick the bucket) are part of Source and yet they continue to be themselves. Make sense?

Each one of us has the capability to do what Esther is able to do, because we are all drops that come from that great ocean.

Esther is an auditory translator of the information she reaches for from the ocean that is Source – all this means is that she translates the energy of Source through words. Other people have the ability to translate information from Source in the form of visions, color or light, or in the form of feelings and emotions that they feel, or sounds that they hear in their heads.

Esther receives from Source complete thoughts and she then finds words to express these thoughts. It is exactly the same process that an artist uses to create a piece of art, or a musician uses to write an inspired piece of music or an author such as my self uses when we feel inspired to write.

From my own experience, I know that the words just flow. I never create outlines of books or prepare slides for my webinars, because I don't create them and then find the information to fill in the space – I just begin with the intention of writing or speaking and use my words to translates the thoughts that I am receiving either as I write or as I speak.

We all have the ability to maintain our individual earthly perspective or to don the perspective of Source and see

15

the world and everything in it through the eyes of God or Source. You can give these two perspectives two separate names or not – it doesn't matter. I promise you that all of us switch between these two perspectives many times during our day; and some of us learn to make that shift intentionally while for most others the shift takes place without them knowing it.

"You are creator; you create with your every thought."
~ Abraham

What does Source want?

The objective of Source is the growth of the Universe.

How does the Universe grow?

The Universe grows with the creation of new matter in the form of energy – thought energy.

We humans are thinking machines, churning out thought energy that contributes towards the growth of the Universe.

Every time we think a thought we manufacture new energy, and the objective of Source is fulfilled. Whether we get what we want or not, with each thought we think the universe expands and grows.

The more we think a thought the more energy we send to a subject and the more energy we send to a subject the more it begins to take physical form.

Technically speaking, whether we think happy thoughts or unhappy thoughts – a thought is a thought and it is energy. So despite the fact that there is suffering in the world, the Universe is expanding and its purpose is being served.

The Earth we live on was thought into place by the Thinkers. Abraham says that in the beginning there was a thought and then the thought became the thinker. Everything starts out as a thought and thoughts become manifest. The Earth with everything that is on it was created as a place where more thoughts would be thought that would lead to the expansion of the universe. It was never Source's objective to create suffering in the world. Life was supposed to be good. Experience contrast to give birth to desire, and think that desire into manifestation and feel joyful – that was the intended cycle of creation.

"You are not here to prove worthiness; you are here to extend creation."
~ Abraham

Why does Abraham want to help us?

Source benefits from the expansion and growth of the universe that is a result of our churning out thoughts, and Source would much rather that this expansion was the result of happy thoughts rather than unhappy thoughts, because life is meant to feel good.

The human history of the world has seen many prophets like Abraham bring the message of God to man in an effort to end all suffering. If the objective of Source is served whether we get what we want or not, then why not assist in the expansion of the universe while having fun along the way getting what we want, rather than suffering through the journey. That is why Abraham bring us their teachings – teachings that can help us in enjoying the journey, teachings that have the potential of spreading joy in the world, teachings that help us to understand how the universe works.

That's what Abraham's work is: to help us on our journey so that we can enjoy being alive.

Experiencing different situations in the word is meant to feel good, we are supposed to get everything we want.

We are supposed to live life with joy. We are supposed to be free to choose whatever we want. Abraham's teachings focus on helping us remember how to use our internal guidance system so that we can live a happy and fulfilled life.

"The basis of your life is freedom; the purpose of your life is joy".
~ Abraham

The hot seat experience

Abraham-Hicks workshops are held in many cities of the USA as well as other countries. Abraham starts the workshop by giving an introduction that lays the foundation for the day to come. This gets the vibration in the room going. Then Abraham invites questions from the audience, and they pick from people who raise their hands those who "**light up**". These are people whose desire to get an answer is at its height and their propensity to hear the answer is also high – they are "**in the vicinity of the vortex**". They are people who will present the question that many in the room are asking, in the best possible way.

One by one people are called up to a chair "**the hot seat**" and Abraham answers their questions.

Abraham promise that whether you get into the hot seat or not, if you bring a question to the workshop it will be answered – I believe them because I have experienced this when I have attended Abraham workshops myself.

Abraham answers the vibrational questions and not just the question that is being asked in words. Sometimes, it appears to the people listening that Abraham is not answering the question that was asked, yet everyone who comes to the hot seat leaves completely satisfied because Abraham addresses the real question – the question that is held in the heart.

"Our work is about helping you how it is that you are Creator and how you go about it deliberately. Because until you do it deliberately you are not fulfilling your reason for being here."
~ Abraham

Manifesting

Manifesting is the process of getting what you want, so that it is a knock on wood reality in the physical world. In an ideal situation, we would give birth to a desire and it would manifest. For example, I feel like eating a mango, and in a few minutes, hours or days, a friend might drop by with a basket of mangoes, or I might walk into the grocery store and find mangoes on sale, or I might run into someone giving away free samples. Abraham says that none of these are coincidences. When we ask for something or desire it, and our **desire is pure** (meaning that there is no resistance towards it), then the universe will orchestrate a series of events which will bring us the thing we want. There are many possible ways in which the object of our desire can come into our life; we can't see all the possibilities, but the Universe is aware of all of them. So if we were to simply allow the Universe to guide us, rather than try to figure out a way to get to the things we want, life would be much more satisfying for us. Instead most of us try to figure things out, playing with pros and cons and giving rise to worry and anxiety, which take away the fun and joy that is supposed to be ours.

Most people start learning about the law of attraction so that they can manifest the things that they want. Abraham says that all things that we want are possible.

"If you can think it, you can have it."
~ Abraham

Resistance & Beliefs

Resistance, is the "lack of believability factor", which makes us feel that our desire is impossible or inappropriate. When we feel this way, we create an obstruction due to which it takes longer for the manifestation. The more the resistance, the longer and harder it becomes to get the object of our desire.

Abraham uses an analogy to explain resistance. They talk about a cork like the one used to close bottles with. If you throw a cork like that into a pail of water, it floats on the surface, because that is its natural tendency. It will never sink to the bottom of the pail. In order for the cork to sink to the bottom of the pail you will need to hold it down with force. The weight of that force is the resistance that the cork has to push against in order to get back to the surface. Abraham says that the easiest way to get rid of resistance is to just let it go – let go the hand that is holding the cork down and the cork will rise to the surface in no time at all. Similarly, the minute we give up our resistance on a subject, we can move forward towards getting what we want.

"The way to speed up manifestation is to get resistance out of the way."
~ Abraham

Resistance is often a result of our **Beliefs**. Most times our beliefs are so deep seated that we would not be able to articulate them even if we wanted to. For example, if I believed that mangoes were not in season and therefore, it would be impossible for me to get any at this time, then that would be my reality, and I would want mangoes but none would come to me. The manifestation of my desire would be pushed out in time to the coming of the mango season.

"The Art of Allowing is wanting so much to feel good, that whether you are pursuing the past or the present or the future, you're deliberately looking for the best feeling thought that you can find."
~ Abraham

We tend to pick up beliefs from observing the experience of other people, or accepting their opinion about a situation. Many of our beliefs are picked up during childhood. So if my mother had told me that mangoes could only be had in the mango season and I accepted this as true under all conditions, then that belief would become the framework that would determine my reality. I would have ruled out all other possibilities.

However, if my beliefs were softer, in the sense that I was open to the idea that there could be other ways of getting mangoes out of season, now, I might find a tin of mangoes abandoned by the roadside, and so on – you get the drift?

Every time, we see something or hear something and accept it as a given, we create a belief about it. When we accept a thought, law of attraction brings us more of it – this proves our belief right. Every time our belief is proven right it becomes stronger. Every time a belief is proven right, law of attraction will present us with more opportunities to observe the evidence of it. Therefore, **a belief is a thought we think again and again**.

We activate a belief by focusing on it. At any given time we have countless active and inactive beliefs.

If you took paper and pen and decided to make a list of all your beliefs, you would have a hard time doing it, mainly because most people are unaware of what constitutes a belief.

Empowering beliefs create a habit of thought that is empowering. Negative beliefs create a habit of thought that is disempowering.

"If you want to change what you are living, you only have to change the way you are thinking."
~ Abraham

Three Steps to Manifesting

Abraham says that manifesting the things that we want is a three step process:

Step One: A desire is born, we ask for things we want, by thinking about them. The birthing of a desire is usually born out of our experience of the world and wanting things to be different.

Step Two: Source answers and the thing you want is Vibrationally created (explained later), and held for you in a vibrational escrow that Abraham calls the vortex (explained later).

Step Three: We allow our creation into our lives and a manifestation takes place.

"I get what I think about – wanted or not."
~ Abraham

Abraham says that Step One is part of human nature. As we see the world around us we decide what we **prefer** and therefore give birth to desires. Source always answers. Whatever we ask for – it is always given, every time. Whether it appears in our life experience in the form of hard, knock on wood reality is a function of how easy we are about it, what sort of belief systems we have, and the level of resistance we have accumulated.

More recently, Abraham has introduced **Step Four**: holding your vibration in a better place, recognizing when you're not there and doing the work using the processes Abraham talks about such as meditation, appreciation, and sleep to regain alignment. Life is good when we live mostly in Step Four. Once we learn how to use Abraham's processes, all it takes is practice to get to Step Four and stay there. It's just like riding a bike. When you first start trying to ride a bike, you fall off but eventually you start getting the idea, and maintain your balance so that you can ride smoothly.

Rockets of Desire

Abraham uses the term "rockets of desire" all the time. A rocket of desire is the moment of the birthing of a new desire, this process causes a spike in our energy level and Abraham describes this as a rocket, because the energy spike emanates from our bodies like a fireworks rocket. If we were translators of energy at Abraham's level we would be able to see these rockets. The spike of energy happens because when we birth a desire we feel good even if it is only for a split second and that's when the rocket of energy rises. Then we feel the absence of the object of our desire and go down the emotional scale.

In a workshop setting where Abraham calls people up, they select people on the basis of reading this sort of energy spike. Abraham says that the energy spike makes people stand out and that is how they are called to the "hot seat".

When a fresh desire is born the moment of birthing is a micro second of being in a place of feeling the joy from wanting something that you want. It's only the next second when past beliefs kick in and you move your focus from the pure desire to the lack of it and the impossibility of getting it that pushes it away. This means that if you could stay in that vibration of joy experienced at the birthing of the desire, then the desire would manifest immediately.

"I'll give up all my misery for the joy that is natural to me – because I can't have both."
~ Abraham

Like attracts like

Abraham says that "like" vibrations attract.

We attract people and events that are at the same level as our level on the emotional scale.

Therefore, if I am feeling frustrated, and I want to vent my frustration, it is not possible for me to meet up with a friend who at that time is in the vibration of joy on the emotional scale (explained in detail later). I will attract someone else who is Vibrationally at the level of frustration.

Let's say I call the phone company for help with my cell phone, I am more likely to get on the phone with a tech rep who is less than competent or less than courteous. Whereas if I call the same company when I am in a state of joy, I will get a tech rep who is both courteous and competent. I might even attract these qualities out of someone who is not always like that, but my experience with them would be of the best kind.

This is why it is so important to maintain our vibration in the feeling of joy, love and hope, because these are the best feeling emotions that we as humans have access to. When we feel good, good things happen. When we feel bad we attract things that make us feel worse into our lives. Abraham teaches us to feel the feeling of joy without wanting things to change before we feel good. In other words, don't put your joy on hold waiting for things to change.

"Every time you spend time looking at something unwanted, you just practice the vibration that attracts it to you."
~ Abraham

Thought forms and Creations: Vibrational Reality

Thoughts are a form of energy. Once a thought is thought, it is energized and it never goes away, because energy can only change shape, it cannot be destroyed.

The human brain is the most advanced brain among all living things. We think and birth more desires than any other living thing, and as we think we energize our thoughts – this is the creative process. This is how we create things.

We create things by giving energy to them. Once we create something, it always exists. The more we think upon a subject the more energy we give it. We give it positive energy when we think of it from a happy place and this makes it manifest. When we think of it from a lower emotional place, we keep it from manifesting for us, however, it has been created and therefore it is a **vibrational reality or a thought form**.

I love the example of Star Trek. All the wonderful gadgets created by the screenplay author were thought of and therefore they became a vibrational reality. Then, several generations of people from all over the world watched the program and wondered at the creations, they thought about them (mostly without any resistance), they dreamt about them, they talked about them, they wondered how wonderful it would be to have them, and as a result they all gave more and more energy to the vibrational reality – so that eventually the gadgets started becoming a manifested reality. No one who watched Star Trek, had sufficiently resistant thoughts to the creation of these gadgets so there was no obstruction to the creation – just the collective human belief that the technology needed had not been developed. This belief propelled many scientists and inventors to asking the question "what is needed to create these gadgets?" and the answers have been coming to us over a period of time.

Abraham says that there are **"rivers of thought"**, because thoughts of a similar nature are attracted to each other. This is how things become mainstream from being remote. We see this often in fashion or in the colloquial use of language.

All humans are translators of energy. We are all equipped with five energy translation mechanisms – our five senses. Our senses collect information from our environment so that we can establish our preferences and gain clarity about what we truly want. All of this information translates into the way we feel, and the emotions that we feel as a result are indicators of what we should do in order to get what we prefer.

"You train your perception to translate the world".
~ Abraham

Energy, rivers of thought and thought forms

There is no such thing as the ghost of the person that once lived. However, people who are able to read vibration or energy are able to tune themselves to the thought forms and the rivers of thought that exist all around us.

To see the ghost of someone, simply means that you are tapping into the thoughts that the person thought when they were alive and interpreting them with your visual sensory mechanism. Some people interpret thought forms through the sense of hearing, or smelling or touching.

Let's say that someone had lost a key while alive and now that they have transitioned, another can "see" their ghost still looking for the keys, that simply means that they are tapping into the thought form of looking for lost keys – it does not mean that the soul of the transitioned person is banging around still looking for the keys and not finding peace in the process.

Rivers of thought that keep attracting other similar thoughts because people continue to think these thoughts gather momentum. Continued focus keeps energizing things until they manifest. Through the power of focus thoughts are born and through the power of continued focus they manifest. This is the process through which the universe was created. The earth was thought upon by thinkers until it took form.

Thoughts of a similar kind and at the same emotional frequency level band together, so every thought that has ever been thought about the devil for example, bands into a river of thought. People who are in a place of fear and have belief systems that suggests that there is a devil will tap into this river of thought and receive from it. So is the devil real? Yes, absolutely. The devil is a thought form, thought into place by all the people who believe in its existence. There is no source of evil but there does exist a river of thoughts, thought by people that believe in it. Those who live their lives in Step Four cannot have access to such rivers of thought because they are living their lives on an emotional frequency level that cannot match up with that.

"When you feel good only good things can come to you".
~ Abraham

Contrast

Contrast is what gives birth to desire. When we observe the world around us and determine our preference about how we would like things to be, we are giving birth to desire, from the experience of contrast.

The "having of", and the "lack of" are contrasting situations. When we have something and we wish to improve it, we are feeling contrast. When we don't have something then we are feeling contrast.

There is always contrast in the world. The process of night following day, the seasons following each other, all help us to identify our preferences. Our five physical senses perform the same function, helping us to sift through our environment and determine what we like and what we do not like.

Simply put, contrast is the distance between what we like and what we do not like. The experiencing of contrast is different for each of us because of our preferences and our perspectives. For example, air temperature of 15 degrees Celsius might be considered cold by someone from the Middle East who is used to experiencing temperatures of 57 degrees in the summer, but for someone living in Canada, 15 degrees is very pleasant weather.

Contrast makes us look at things in different ways and determine our preferences. When we give birth to a preference we give birth to a desire to have things the way we prefer them.

The yin-yang symbol is a perfect depiction of contrast, and the fact that we are always in control of our choice or decision to put our focus on one aspect of the situation.

"If you are a creator and we promise you, you are, and if what a creator is, is one who flows energy, then what could be better than an environment where it is very clear what is not wanted."
~ Abraham

The Emotional Scale

At any point in time, we can tell how free flowing our connection with Source is based upon how we feel. In the book "Ask & it is Given", by Esther and Jerry Hicks, Abraham has described the "**Emotional Scale**".

The emotional scale consists of 22 different emotions that go from despair at the lower energy end to joy at the higher energy end. It is important to know that the stages from "hope" to "joy" are part of the **Vortex**. A summary scale is depicted below, for a complete listing of the various levels please refer to the book "Ask & it is Given".

The Emotional Scale

| Fear | Anger | Worry | Frustration | Hope | Joy |

Hi ← — Resistance — → Lo

A point on the emotional scale is called a **set-point**. Therefore, there are 22 set-points.

You can identify where you are on the emotional scale by asking yourself questions. The first point of differentiation is to know if you are feeling generally good or generally bad and then find out which specific level you are at. The only reason you might want to know more specifically is for the purpose of selecting one of the processes given in the book to improve your vibration. Abraham has prescribed certain processes as being more useful for the different stages of the emotional scale. Other than that, there is really no reason to delve more precisely into where you are on the emotional scale, because from where ever you are your objective is always to feel even better.

More recently, Abraham has been talking about only two emotions: that which feels **good** and that which does **not feel good**. That is all we need to identify.

Processes are thinking exercises that Abraham teaches. The purpose of these exercises is to help us improve our vibration so that we can move towards a place of joy on the emotional scale.

"Feel your way forward."
~ Abraham

Alignment or lining up

Alignment is an emotional place. When we are in a state of alignment we are living life from the higher levels of the emotional scale, which means that we have very low or no resistance towards manifesting things and events that we desire. That is why when we are in a state of alignment all things that we want manifest for us with ease.

A general feeling of alignment feels "good". It feels as if all things are working out and the universe has our back. Being in alignment makes life easy and fun.

Alignment =   Moving up the emotional scale towards love and joy.

Alignment =   Ease and flow, and the absence of resistance.

Alignment =   The belief that what we want is possible.

Alignment =   Being one with Source and your Inner-being.

Alignment =   Feeling good.

Abraham often refers to alignment using the expression "alignment with Source". When we are in alignment, we are inside the vortex (explained later).

The process of creation involves feeling contrast and giving birth to desire, then finding alignment with the desire in order to manifest it.

Abraham often uses the term "lining up" as a substitute for the word alignment, usually in the context of lining up with Source or lining up with your Inner-being – meaning think about a topic in the same way that Source is thinking about it in that moment in time. When we don the perspective of Source we feel good and when our perspective differs from that of Source we feel bad (negative emotion).

"If you had only one goal, and that was to feel good, you would live successfully and happily, and in a way of fulfilling your life's purpose – ever after."
~ Abraham

Inner-being

Abraham says that all of us have an Inner-being, who is non-physical. Our Inner-being is the "**greater part of us**". We are the physical extension of this Inner-being. The Inner-being is a consciousness, and all Inner-beings collectively form Source or the Universe, or collective consciousness.

This collective consciousness has the ability to focus as One, or as Several. At any point in time Source, can see through the eyes of a bee and simultaneously through the eyes of a human. All Inner-beings are connected and have complete information about everything. All seeing, All knowing, All powerful.

When we are in alignment with our Inner-being we "**see through the eyes of Source**".

An Inner-being can have more than one physical consciousness emanating from it at any time. The lifetime that you are experiencing is just one point of focus or one perspective that your Inner-being is focusing through; it is also simultaneously focused through other people and other living things. So your

Inner-being is much bigger than you are, and that is why Abraham refers to it as "the greater part of you".

It can also have access to any other physical consciousness through other Inner-beings. When we are aligned with our Inner-being we have access to all that our Inner-being has access to. That's what **genius** is – the ability to connect so completely with our Inner-being that we draw from it the knowledge that is available to Source through the collective intelligence of All-That-Is. Everything that has ever been lived or ever been thought is accessible to us through our alignment with our Inner-being, because all that is once created or thought exists for ever.

Abraham also says that when you feel bad or uncomfortable, that is an emotional indicator that your Inner-being does not agree with your perspective. So if you encounter someone and come away thinking that that person does not like you, and you feel bad; the reason that you feel bad is not because that person doesn't like, you feel bad because your Inner-being disagrees with your opinion. Inner-being never takes a negative perspective, and so while you feel disliked, your Inner-being knows that the Inner-being of that other person loves you, and your Inner-being loves that other person regardless. Inner-being and Source want us to come to all situations with unconditional love. When you are feeling and flowing love you are in a place of alignment. When you are aligned everything around you feels good.

If you make a decision and then feel bad about it, what that means is that your Inner-being knows that you can make that decision work in your favor. Your Inner-being never sees you as being down and out; Inner-being always sees you as being powerful and having the ability to have, be or do anything you want. Inner-being feels that no matter what decision you make things can always work out in your favor, because Inner-being is always there to guide you to your greater good. To hear this guidance you must be in a place of alignment.

"Consciousness does not need physical form, but physical form needs consciousness, and consciousness enjoys physical form, because physical form is the leading edge of thought. So consciousness expands through the physical form. It's not one or the other."
~ Abraham

The Leading Edge of Creation

We humans, are described by Abraham as the **"leading edge of creation"**. This is because, the process of creation of anything, whether it is a physical object, a relationship, a bodily condition or an event, everything starts with the identification of contrast and the giving birth to desire. There is no living or non-living thing on the surface of this Earth that feels contrast in the amount of detail that we humans do, and give birth to intensity of desire in the same way that we do. Humans are the peak performing "thinking" machines, churning out new thought energy and contributing to the expansion of the universe. If we did not give birth to new desires, then nothing new would be created in the universe. The evolution of species, the evolution of technologies – all progress depends upon this process. Therefore, without the human ability to focus and think life on planet Earth would come to a standstill.

There is consciousness in every particle of the universe, down to the atoms and the sub-atomic particles that constitute all matter. Where ever there is consciousness, there is thought, and thought is at the basis of the expansion and growth of the universe. That which we call inanimate is also made up of particles of matter that carry consciousness, but the role of that consciousness is not to discern, it is to serve, and even though it is also asking for continual improvement, it is not collecting information from its environment and using it to discern it's preferences – so it is more or less passive. As we go up the ladder of living things on the Earth, the level of consciousness increases culminating in the humans. For example, trees are consciousness too, but animals are more "feeling" in comparison and humans are more "feeling" than animals.

The more we feel, the more we decide on our preferences and the more we ask for improvement – and that whole process of feeling, deciding and asking is based on thinking thoughts.

"You are on the leading edge of thought, taking thought beyond that which it has been before."
~ Abraham

The Purpose of life and Expansion of the Universe

The purpose of life is joyful expansion. Expansion is the creation of new things, events, relationships, bodily conditions etc.

The process of creation is supposed to be joyful for us. Yet, many of us for much of our lives do nothing but bang around in contrast without manifesting. Manifesting is the ultimate completion of the creation process. Joy is in the experiencing of the process. We are supposed to enjoy giving birth to new desires and the process that gets us to them. There was never meant to be any suffering in the world.

Suffering or pain is just an indication of resistance which is blocking our alignment with our Inner-being. When we trust our Inner-being and we trust Source and understand the process of creation, then we know that there is nothing to worry about. That life is easy and that we can have be or do anything we want – that is what **"faith"** is.

The "**joy is in the journey**" towards our creation, because once we actually get that thing that we want our joy is complete, and then it is gone and we're on to wanting and creating the next thing. Life never stands still because we are always giving birth to new desires and on our way to them.

Abraham says that the ultimate test of how well we are using the law of attraction is the reality we are living in the Now. If we like what we are living then it is a confirmation of the fact that we are thinking thoughts that are conducive to our joy, and if we are dis-satisfied with the life we are living then it is proof of the fact that the way we are thinking our thoughts is not serving us, because it is not leading us to joy.

"Physical experience provides an object of attention through which Non-physical energy can flow."
~ Abraham

There is no death – you are alive and alive

There is no death but there is a process of transitioning from the physical body. Death is a change of focus – rather than see things from our own individual focus we start to see the bigger picture or the perspective of our Inner-being and that of Source. In other words, the drop of water becomes one with the ocean. When this transition occurs, the point of focus that is us is withdrawn by our Inner-being into itself. Nothing that we have ever lived is lost, it is still there and the point of focus that is us is still able to activate all of who we are but without the resistance that might have been part of the physical individual.

In order to connect with a point of focus that we know as a loved one who has transitioned we need to be in a state of alignment. As Abraham says "look for them where they now are, rather than look for them where they are not". When we look for a transitioned loved one from a position of missing them, we are looking for them from the perspective of lack, and a perspective of lack creates resistance towards the attainment of our desire to connect with them or to feel the presence of them in our lives.

Abraham says that all death is suicide because the decision to withdraw focus is made at the level of the Inner-being who is part of us. Inner-being will withdraw focus from a physical body when there is no fun associated with creation through that specific focus, when there is no feeling of contrast or when the contrast felt and the resistance accumulated as a result is so great that the human existence cannot overcome the feeling of despair.

Abraham encourages us to be at peace with the transition that is death, because the Inner-being never dies, and the point of focus that is us never loses its existence. We never forget our life on planet Earth or our loved ones, or the things we loved to do and we are always interested in those subjects and always participating in them through the eyes and senses of those others who are currently focused and experiencing them. So someone like a great composer such as Mozart remains interested in the creation of music by those who are now on planet Earth and engaged in the creation of new pieces of music. My mother remains interested in my well-being. No one who has ever lived, goes away as a result of physical death.

Past Life Regression

When we tap into Source or our Inner-being the information that we get could be about us or it could be about anyone else. Once a life is lived, the details of that life experience are available to all Inner-beings that collectively form Source. There is no separation. From our narrow perspective in this physical body it is not possible for us to know if the vision we are getting is from one of the lives focused by our Inner-being or any other Inner-being. When we re-emerge into Non-physical, it doesn't matter because from that perspective the purpose is the collective expansion of the universe and collective knowing of all things.

Abraham says that what we extract during a past life regression depends on where we are on the emotional scale – because like vibration attracts like vibration, so the images and information that we extract is indicative of the emotional place we hold at that point in time. It provides information about our emotional trajectory and is indicative of our manifestational direction, but in no way is there any certainty that the images we see are from a life that was focused by our inner-being or any other inner-being.

The Vortex

The vortex is the term Abraham uses to denote that place where all our vibrational creations accumulate as they are waiting to manifest. The vortex is a non-physical, vibrational place – it is a feeling place. It is where the first step of manifestation takes place – at this first step the manifestation is in vibrational form – it can be felt but it cannot be interpreted using the five physical senses.

The vortex is the place where the Inner-being resides. When we are in alignment we are in the vortex with our Inner-being and all the things that we wish to manifest. From inside the vortex, we see things the way Source or Inner-being sees them.

No one stays inside the vortex for ever – because the creation process takes place from outside the vortex – new desires are born from experiencing contrast mostly outside the vortex. Step One, is mostly outside the vortex. Step Two is the Inner-being responding. Step Three, is inside the vortex alignment with our Inner-being. Manifestation occurs in Step Three.

Those who are used to spending most of their time inside the vortex feel contrast a lot more when they come out of the vortex than those who have become accustomed to the lower energies. When you are used to things going well mostly, the contrast of things not going your way is a lot bigger.

The higher energy levels on the emotional scale are inside the vortex – all the way from hope to joy.

All our preferences are stored in the vortex. As we observe the world and decide what we prefer, we might forget our preference, but our Inner-being never forgets. Let's say you observed how your parents interacted with each other and you decided what aspects of this interaction you liked and what aspects you did not like, you might have forgotten all of those thoughts as an adult – but your Inner-being never forgets – it knows and will take all of those preferences into account as well as all the other preferences you have ever thought on this subject when it matches you up with someone.

The vortex is a sorting mechanism that assembles within it all the **cooperative components** required in order to produce a manifestation. That is why we have to get into the vortex in order for our request to be completed, as we are also one of the cooperative components. At any one point in time the vortex has a selection of components ready and available to complete the creation process. What we want can come about in many different ways and the universe always has a number of possibilities lined up for the way things will unfold.

In the above example of looking for a mate, your Inner-being will at all times know who matches up with all your preferences at all times – today it might be person X, and tomorrow X might have moved on and your Inner-being will have person Y lined up who also matches up exactly with all your preferences. So at any point in time, there will always be a suitable person in your vortex, and soon as you get into the vortex you will be matched up with the person who at that moment is in the vortex with you, and matches where you are at an energetic level on the emotional scale. There is no one answer to any question, no unique best fit for any situation – the possibilities are constantly changing.

This explains why people fall out of love with each other – their preferences change, and their energetic level on the emotional scale also changes. The only way people stay together is because despite these changes they continue to find things to appreciate about each other and continue feeling the feeling of love for each other.

At one of the workshops Abraham offered a wonderful analogy about the Vortex. They said that the vortex is pregnant with all the things that you have created, and the process of giving birth is like the process of manifesting. Just like you know that the baby is in the womb, and you accept that it exists without actually seeing it, so if you could believe that all things you have created are in the vortex and will manifest when you line up with them, then there would be ease in the process of manifesting. The easiest path to a happy and fulfilled life is to believe that the moment you express a desire it is granted and it is only a matter of time before it will manifest – that the manifestation is a confirmed event.

Abraham says that we are all in the vortex or in the vicinity of it at some point of time in our day. When something makes us happy, and even if it is for a split second, during that split second we are in the vortex. The trick is to recognize when we are there and then to **"milk it"**, meaning, introduce more subjects that make you happy so that you extend the time period that you are in the vortex.

At one seminar, Abraham mentioned that if we could be in the vortex more compared to the times we were out, then all things that we wanted would work out for us.

Our manifested reality is a measure of how aligned we are. If we are mostly living the life we want then we are mostly aligned. If we are living a life that we are not happy or satisfied with then we are mostly not in alignment.

Understanding the concept of the vortex is key to the understanding of the teachings of Abraham.

"If you have an out of the vortex vibration going on your life will reflect it."
~ Abraham

The Spinning Grid Discs and Momentum

The grid is the *framework of reality* into which our manifestations flow. This framework is made up of our *beliefs* and our *expectations* and is powered by the *momentum* of our thinking. Our vibrational creations flow from the Vortex into the Grid, in other words, they flow from vibrational reality to manifestational reality.

The more you focus on a subject or think about it, the more you "*energize*" it and the more momentum it has. You activate and de-activate beliefs by thinking about them and including them in your mix or excluding them. The more times you think a thought the more energy it has and the more momentum it has to pull you along with it. So if you mostly think enabling thoughts then the momentum of being able to achieve is greater in your life, and if you think thoughts of difficulty then those thoughts have momentum and you will encounter difficulty.

We are in control and therefore we can shift our focus at any point in time and change momentum. However, it is much easier to change momentum in the early stages when acceleration hasn't really started. Abraham has used the ***analogy of the car going downhill*** to explain. If a car is pushed downhill, but you get ahead of it before it gathers speed, you can stop it where it is and change its direction. But once the car has started rolling it gathers speed and now it cannot be stopped, and you cannot get ahead of it because if you do you will be crushed by the momentum – ***crash and burn*** as Abraham puts it.

Let's continue with the example of looking for a job, say you think a negative thought for the very first time "interviews are difficult because interviewers are trying to find fault with me so that they can reject me as a potential hire". Then you think "I really know my stuff, and when they talk to me they will be able to see that I really am the best person for this job". It is easy to differentiate one of these thoughts as being on a negative momentum disc and the other being on a positive momentum disc. Whichever one of these thoughts you think most often will determine which of your discs has the most momentum (is spinning at a higher speed), and that one will determine the results of your interview. Make sense? So every moment can be a different grid because you can choose to think a different thought. The thought is the grid, and it is backed up by your beliefs and expectations. If you think the same thought again and again, it gains momentum and the grid underlying the thought is the grid that *"fills-in"* with manifestation.

The analogy of the spinning grid disc combines the philosophy of the emotional scale with that of momentum and focus. The speed at which the grid disc is spinning is reflective of the momentum that it has gathered. The actual grid consists of beliefs and focus. Imagine a that you have a stack of frisbees to play with. Each frisbee (grid disc) is representative of a subject that is important to you in your life. So you have a frisbee about the subject of employment, one about the ease of money flowing in, another about how good you are at cooking a roast, one about the personality of your friend Joe, and another about how coffee tastes at the café around the corner. You have a grid disc or frisbee about each subject in your life. Each frisbee is made up of a crisscross pattern of beliefs. Criss are the beliefs that are empowering or make you feel good, and Cross are the beliefs that are negative and make you feel bad. It is your decision which beliefs to focus on and activate. Every time you think about the subject of your frisbee, you are throwing the frisbee into the air. These Frisbees are unique in the sense that they store inside them the energy that you use to throw them each time. So if you activate negative beliefs when you throw the frisbee, negative energy gets stored and when you activate positive beliefs, positive energy gets stored. The more energy is stored on the disc the faster it spins. If you have more positive momentum then your Frisbee is headed in the direction of what you want with greater speed. If you activate positive beliefs some of the time and negative beliefs some of the time, you have what Abraham calls "split energy". When you are splitting your energy it takes a lot longer to get to the things you want. If you activate negative beliefs more often than positive beliefs you may end up getting the opposite of what you want.

"Do your affirming from a high-flying disc."
~ Abraham

The Wobble and Conditions

In 2014 Abraham started using a new term the "wobble". We all know what a wobble is? A chair wobbles when its legs are not equally balanced. A top wobbles when it loses its momentum and is about to come to a stop. A grid disc wobbles when it has both positive and negative momentum going on at the same time. A wobble is an indication of lack of balance or alignment or split energy.

Abraham says that wanting the things around you (conditions) to change so that you can feel good introduces a wobble in your vibration – this disrupts your trajectory towards the things that you want. Think about it, if a Frisbee wobbles in the air, it falls very quickly to the ground – it loses its momentum and can miss its target.

The question is, why does wanting conditions to change create a wobble? The answer is, because when you want something to change you are emitting a vibration of dissatisfaction – what frequency do you think that is? Dissatisfaction is a negative vibration, and when you emit a negative vibration you cannot get a positive result – because like attracts like. Instead of wanting conditions to change so we can feel good, what would

benefit us is making peace with the way things are –
accepting them as they are and acknowledging that
change for the better is possible, then turning our
attention to things we can appreciate, and putting one
hundred percent of our power of focus there.

*"I am introducing wobble because I'm trying to
get you to agree with me rather than aligning
with what already agrees with me – Source
agrees with me. Why are you looking at
humans for your alignment when Source is
right here beaming it at you all the time."
~ Abraham*

The receptive mode

More recently Abraham has been using the term "the receptive mode" to mean being in the vortex or in the vicinity of the vortex – or the higher levels of the emotional scale.

You have to be in the receptive mode in order for solutions to come to you. When you're not in the receptive mode you are in the vibration of the question. When we ask a question or birth a desire we are in Step One. When we are in the vibration of the solution or getting the manifestation we are in Step Three. Being in the receptive mode is being in Step Three. The receptive mode is the mode of receiving.

All our work is to focus our thoughts on things that feel good, because that is how we raise our vibration and when we raise our vibration we go up the emotional scale and that's when we get into the receptive mode.

"I can be happy anytime I decide to turn my attention towards that which connects me with my Source of joy."
~ Abraham

17 Seconds, to 68 Seconds, to Creation

Abraham has said on many occasions that 17 seconds of thinking a thought activates it, so that another thought with similar energy on the emotional scale will follow it, and then another and another. So 17 seconds of thinking a positive thought attracts another positive thought and another, and 17 seconds of focus on a negative thought brings another like it and so on. Within 68 seconds of a train of thought enough momentum has been created that it can have an impact on the manifestation you want. A negative train will have a negative impact and a positive train will have a positive impact.

If you were actually spending 17 seconds on a singular thought, only four successive thoughts would take you to the 68 second mark.

That is why having a positive habit of thought is so important. The way you think is the way you think – and if you are used to looking at the glass half full then that is the way you attempt life and if you are used to looking at the glass half empty then that is your habit of thought. As a result, those who think things are hard, take that habit of thought to everything they do and things become harder for them as a result.

As I coach people, and hear them speak, I notice that most people have no idea what their habit of thought is. They all want positive results in their life and therefore they believe that they are positive thinking, but in reality the way they articulate their thoughts is indicative of their beliefs and many times this is a negative way of coming to the subject.

"Everyone is creating, because everyone is thinking."
~ Abraham

Co-creation

Abraham uses the expression co-creation to signify the process of creation that involves more than one individual.

We are always co-creating. Everyone that we come across during our day is part of our co-creation. We co-create with animals as well as other humans.

I have heard Abraham say that the process of co-creation is the process of birthing of desires, however the manifesting of desires is an individual thing.

We enjoy life through co-creating with others. We are co-creating in all our relationships. We attract co-creators to ourselves based on the spinning grid disc on which we are or our frequency on the emotional scale. Therefore, the people or co-creators we attract are a reflection of our point of attraction. For example, if you are feeling prosperous you will attract the company of others who are like you. It reminds me of the fact that my mother always used to say "you become like the company you keep".

"People have trained you to care about how they think, because it's important to most people who are living conditionally for you to create conditions that they can live with. There is an endless trap in that."
~ Abraham

In relationships that are more binding like that of a child with a parent or a spouse with a spouse, our co-creators may not always be on the same grid disc as ourselves, but we will draw from them the attitude and behavior that is reflective of our own point of attraction. So a mother who is in an attitude of irritation, will attract to herself a tantrum from a child who is perfectly nice otherwise.

"If you can't trust people to like you, you can't attract people who do."
~ Abraham

Power of Influence

We cannot create in the experience of another, whether that other is another human or an animal, however, we have power of influence over all those we come across and we are subject to their power of influence. Power of influence is simply the setting forth of your intentions with a momentum that is so high that those you co-create with cooperate with your intentions.

"We cannot focus upon the weakness of another and evoke strengths. You cannot focus upon things that you think they are doing wrong, and evoke things that will make you feel better."
~ Abraham

In a co-creative situation, the co-creator with the highest momentum has the most power of influence. Power of influence can be exerted from a good place or not – it can be exerted from any emotional set point on the emotional scale, because it is possible to gather momentum on any grid disc. Our opinions and our expectations about how others will act or react, feel or behave are all beliefs. The stronger our beliefs, the higher the momentum they carry and that is why we will always get what we expect. If we expect someone to be rude – they will be. If you believe that there are crazy drivers on the road, you will find them, and the one who believes that he or she always gets good traffic and easy driving conditions will always manifest those.

"You want to look for someone to love, not for someone who loves you."
~ Abraham

The Stream

I love the analogy of the stream. In fact, it was the first analogy I heard from Abraham.

The current in a stream or a river moves in one direction – downstream. When you put a boat in the water and point it downstream, it takes very little or no effort to get to your destination. When you paddle in a direction opposing the current in the stream, or upstream you have to work really hard because you are working against the power of the current.

Abraham says that it is better to be easy and go with the flow than to try to buck the current. If you go with the flow, the stream will take you where you want to go with less effort.

The power with which the waters flow in the stream is the power of your asking. The more you have been asking for something the faster the waters in your stream are moving and so the harder it is to try to paddle upstream. Going against the current just means that at some point your boat will capsize, or you will get to where you want to go ragged and used up, or you may not get there at all.

In the books "The Astonishing Power of Emotions" and "Ask and it is Given", Abraham teaches us to ask ourselves, "is this an upstream thought or a downstream thought?" and always pick a downstream thought.

It doesn't matter where you put your boat in the stream what's important is that you go with the flow. You could put your boat in at ornery and go downstream pretty soon you wouldn't be ornery anymore. You won't get to joy immediately but you will be going in the right direction – all you need is to feel a little better at a time and not take score. Abraham says that all the things we want are downstream, nothing that we want is upstream. So if something feels hard, chances are that our boat is pointed upstream and we are paddling against the current. All we have to do is to stop trying to paddle against the current and the stream will turn us and take us downstream to where all the things we want are. Going with the stream feels easy, going against the stream feels like a struggle.

"Trust that all is well and look for the evidence of it."
~ Abraham

One who is connected to the stream

From time to time Abraham will call alignment as our connection to the "stream of well-being". They have said on many occasions that one person who is connected to the stream is more powerful than many who are not.

The stream of well-being in this analogy is life itself. The current in the stream is powered by the intensity of our desires and so the more we want things the faster the current flows. In order to get what we want we must go with the flow, because everything that we want is flowing with the current in the stream – fighting the current takes us in the opposite direction from what we want.

One who goes with the current is one who is connected to the stream and is aligned. And one who is aligned is much more powerful that those who are not – because one who is connected to the stream has power of influence over things, people and events around them. It's not that these people control things. It's just that their intentions take everyone around them into its fold. That's why those who are in alignment accomplish more

76

and with greater ease. Things are easy for them, people respond differently to them, paths appear where there were none.

"One who is connected to the stream is more powerful than thousands who are not."
~ Abraham

The Two Ends of a Stick

There are two ways of looking at every subject. The "having of" or "the lack of". It is like the analogy of the "glass half full or the glass half empty". We have the choice of putting our focus on the perspective that we "choose" to don.

Abraham says that we could put all the subjects that are important to us on sticks and pile them up in front of us. Then we could decide which one we want to focus on. We have the power to choose - we could focus on the subjects that are working well or we could focus on the subjects that are not working. If we could choose to focus on the subjects that are working, then by the power of our focus we would be allowing the subjects that are not working to come into alignment. On the other hand, if we choose to focus on the subject that is not working, by the power of that focus we would negatively impact all the other subjects in our life.

"The better it gets, the better it gets – and the worse it gets, the worse it gets."
~ Abraham

The objective is always to focus on those things in our lives that are working. When we focus on things that work, we go up the emotional scale, and the process of going up the emotional scale makes all other things come easily to us. Another way of saying the same thing is that you get more of what you think about in terms of the way it makes you feel. So if you think about things that make you happy you attract more things that will make you happy when they come to you, and when you focus on things that don't make you happy you attract more things that will not make you happy.

Hitting a tree at 5 miles an hour

Abraham used to use this analogy a long time ago, where they would say that hitting a tree when you're in your car going five miles an hour would do much less damage than if you were going 50 miles an hour.

The amount of damage is basically how you're feeling on the emotional scale. If there is a lot of damage then you are probably way down on the scale, perhaps in anger. When the damage is less, you're not as far down on the emotional scale, so let's say for the purpose of this discussion that you are at frustration.

The speed at which you are going is the depth of your desire, if you kinda sorta want something, that's like going five miles an hour, but if you really really want something badly, then you are going at 50 miles an hour.

The tree is the amount of resistance you have built up on the subject of your desire. You could have a very big tree in your way in which case you would have a very serious car crash, or you could have a very small sapling, that doesn't really get in your way very much, just slows you down a bit so that it takes longer to get to your desire, and you feel the bump along the way.

The point Abraham wanted to make with this analogy was that you don't really want to slow down your desire, in order to escape a big car crash. What you want is to remove the trees on your path so that you have an amazing and fast ride getting to the object of your desire.

This analogy was used to explain how people don't want to want things that they feel are impossible to get. That feeling of impossibility is the tree or the resistance. They would much rather not want that much than have to face the disappointment of not getting the object of their desire.

"The way to speed up manifestation is to get resistance out of the way."
~Abraham

Your navigation system is like Magellan

Abraham uses the analogy of the GPS system Magellan, comparing the guidance it gives to drivers to the guidance Source gives us when we are reaching for the things we want.

Just like you need a starting point for your journey towards the things you need, Magellan needs a starting point and a destination point for to plot your course. Magellan does not ask you why you want to go there. Magellan doesn't chastise you when you make a wrong turn, it just recalculates the route. In the same way, Source doesn't ask why you made a wrong turn; Source says, just start from where you are and try again. Just like Magellan doesn't tell you to go back to the starting point of your journey and begin again, Source doesn't tell you to go back and fix your mistakes – just start again from where ever you are. That is why it doesn't matter what has gone past, all that matters is what's next.

When you listen to the guidance that comes from your emotional GPS, it will always lead you in the direction of what you want.

It's important to add that when we feel bad our emotional GPS is telling us that our opinion is different from the opinion of Source about the subject that we are focused on. So let's say you are thinking how much you dislike a certain person, and when you think that thought, it doesn't feel good – that is guidance coming through. What the guidance is telling you is that you are looking at this person in a manner that is different from the way Source is looking at them, because even though you may dislike – Source always loves. This doesn't mean that you have to find a way to love this person, all it means is that you need to find a way to soften your focus by soothing and empowering self-talk.

"This is a universe based on inclusion, "you that I want come to me and you that I don't want – go" and they both come."
~ Abraham

Tuning in to a radio station

Tuning your vibration is likened to tuning in to a radio station. If you want something, you have to tune your vibration to the same level as the thing you want in order for it to come to you. You cannot be tuned to 101 FM and receive 110 AM on that frequency. So if your creation is in the vortex, you must tune to the frequency of the vortex in order to receive what is inside it.

At one workshop Abraham took this analogy further and explained that just like on the old radios you had to keep tuning the dial in order to get a clear reception, so it is with your vibration. Sometimes you get a clear reception, and at other times it's not so great – that is the time to do the work to bring up your vibration so that you can be tuned to the vortex again.

This analogy works really well in explaining the emotional scale. When I heard this analogy from Abraham, I started imagining the emotional scale as a transmission tower, with the various emotions as transmission frequencies. When you transmit at a certain frequency, only those whose radio is tuned to the same frequency can pick up your signal. That is why only they can connect with you. That's why like attracts like. That's why we need to raise our vibration in order to manifest better results.

"You are a vibrational being first, last and always."
~ Abraham

The power of focus and the food buffet

Abraham often uses this analogy. When we go to dine at a buffet, we only put those things on our plate that we wish to partake of – even though there are many choices at the buffet, nothing can land on our plates unless we put it there. Similarly, there are all sorts of things in the world – some that we like and some that we do not like, and with the power of our focus we can filter the things we do not want to include in our life, by not focusing on them.

Whatever we focus on comes to us, whether we say "yes" to it or we say "no" to it. It is the fact that we put our focus on it which magnetizes it and brings it closer and closer to us. The more times we focus on a subject the more it shows up in our lives. Our power of focus is the filtering mechanism that allows us the choice to include things in our life experience or exclude them. The moment we bring a subject into our focus by putting our thoughts on it, it is included in our life experience. If we think of money from the point of view of having it, we get more of it and if we think of money from the point of view of not having it we get more of not having it.

If you looked at poverty and wished that poverty would be removed from the world, you would have magnetized the subject of poverty so now you will see more evidence of it in the world. If you looked at disease and wished there wasn't any, you would magnetize it and now more instances of people who are not well will show up in your life. If you bought a red car and focused on it, now you would see all red cars on the road. So why not use your power of focus to magnetize only those things that you want more of in your experience?

"You get what you think about."
~ Abraham

Falling from an aircraft without a parachute

Sometimes a negative situation continues to get worse, because we are unable to shift our focus from the way things are – so that it gets to a point where things come to a head and there is no turning back. It's like falling out of an air craft without a parachute – there is no way to get back into the air craft and turn things around, we just have to wait for the fall to be over. All we can do is to soften the impact, and we do that by shifting our thoughts.

As Abraham often says "don't worry, it will be over soon". You have to allow the momentum of the situation to run out before you can start again.

An example would be someone who ignores their health to an extent where they finally have a heart attack – they can't undo that, but if they have improved their vibration to some degree (by focusing on watching comedy programs or other things that are fun to think about), it may not be as severe an event - they might be in a train with a doctor sitting right next to them, or they might be right outside the hospital when the pain starts (all examples of softening the impact of the fall).

Abraham says that the futility of the situation actually can be the impetus that makes people give up their resistance. And soon as they give up the resistance, things change. The example Abraham often uses is that of people who have been given the verdict of terminal illness. Some of them, when they receive the verdict give up worrying and fussing about all the things that they were used to worry and fuss about and instead focus on making the most of their time – they focus on the positive side of things and this shift in focus brings about the cure.

"I choose to believe that if I align myself, the right path to all that I want will also be the easiest path to all that I want."
~ Abraham

Laying new pipes

The analogy is based on the experience of the pipes circulating water from the filter to the pond on Esther and Jerry's property being clogged, and the pressure that this created on the pump which continued pumping despite the clog. The clogged pipes could not be cleaned – the only solution to the situation was to lay new pipes.

Abraham has used this analogy to show us how we can deactivate beliefs that no longer serve us. Often it is hard to get rid of a belief, because every time you go to it with the intention of deactivating it; because you bring it up you actually activate it – giving it more power in the process or adding more momentum to it.

This happens often to people who start working with the law of attraction. As they realize that their power of thought is creating their results they try to "fix" their beliefs, but because they don't have enough practice with the techniques that Abraham teaches us, their effort back fires **"all hell breaks loose"** and things start going wrong rather than going right. They give up and go home saying that the law of attraction does not work. Instead, if they took the time to learn the techniques of focus wheeling and segment intending etc, using not the big glaring problems in their lives but little things that they weren't really all that important then they would have the required practice with the techniques and would be able to apply them with success to the big issues in their lives that they want to change. It's like learning to ride a bike – you don't get it right the first time you get on the bike – you fall and get scraped and then you learn how to balance yourself and use the bike. During this process of learning to ride the bike you don't take it out on to the main road – you practice in the park or in your back yard – right?

So fixing is one way to do it, but another way to go is to simply lay new pipes. Rather than try to fix old beliefs, just create new ones that you consciously decide you want. It's like having a really old car that doesn't work anymore, just leave it alone and go get a new one.

Imagine that your communication with Source or your Inner-being was through a pipeline. Imagine that when you asked for something, the message was conveyed to your Inner-being through this pipe. Now imagine that the pipe is clogged due to the resistance and negative beliefs you have built up over time because of the things that haven't been working in your life. Imagine that this obstruction has reduced your pipeline to an extent where only your asking to your Inner-being is getting through, but now the pipeline is one-way traffic only, and even though your Inner-being is answering every time, none of that is coming through to you, so much so that your emotions are dulled and you can't even hear the guidance that your Inner-being is trying to send your way.

Abraham says why not take the easy way out? Why not lay new pipes rather than try to clean the clogged ones?

You lay new pipes by changing your self-talk and making empowering statements. It is better to go general first and make positive statements at a general level and then go specific or talk about the subject upon which you wish to feel an improvement.

Let's say you have a health condition that you want to improve. Over time you have established the belief that your situation is difficult to get over, but you still want an improvement on it. Let's say you have been over the desired weight that you want to be in your physical body. An example of going general and laying new pipes would be to say: "My body knows what to do and does an excellent job on so many things – I don't have to tell my heart how to beat, or my lungs how to breathe. My body is an extension of Source and I believe that the cells of my body are always asking for well-being. I believe that Source is always answering – I believe in well-being." Just don't go to the old pipes that have been laid about weight. The old way of thinking might be "it's so easy for me to put on weight - I eat next to nothing but still I end up gaining more – nothing works for me, I don't like the way I look." Your new pipe has the capacity of creating the body that you want without your ever going to the subject of weight. The only time you would go directly to the subject of weight would be when you would have already started feeling better about the subject. The processes of focus wheeling and segment intending are excellent for this purpose.

"You can only lay new pipes from a high flying disc."
~ Abraham

Pre-paving and Segment Intending

My favorite process. Easy to do and a great habit to have.

Pre-paving involves sending your intentions ahead of you. Setting our intentions about the way we want for things to turn out is the process of consciously creating a reality that we want as opposed to unconsciously submitting to the power of influence of another.

You can pre-pave any segment of time. I like to pre-pave my day while waking up using the process contained in the "Money and Law of Attraction" book by Abraham-Hicks. I also like to pre-pave my sleep time using the night time process given in the same book. I pre-pave my interactions with people. Doing a visualization is also a form of pre-paving the future.

Pre-paving yields to you a reality that is closer to what you intend – the actual results of your pre-paving depend on the momentum you have on the subject and the disc you're on with respect to the emotional scale. If you are too far from the visualization you are creating – it is best to pre-pave a general feeling. For example, if you have no money and you want a new car, just go for the feeling of owning a new car rather than visualizing a specific car. But if you are feeling confident that the new car is within reach then you can get more specific and visualize specific features of the vehicle you are wanting to create.

Many people find it a little confusing to determine when they should go general and when they should get specific. I think that if you are not sure then the best strategy is to stay general. Staying general will always get your there. Getting specific when you are on a high flying disc speeds up the process, but if you are on a low disc, it pushes things further away, because getting specific from a low disc causes the formation of resistance. Stay general for the most part and get specific only when it feels good to do so.

"Every desire that you hatch is possible, not only possible but probable, not only probable it is already done."
~ Abraham

The Book of Positive Aspects

The book of Positive Aspects is one of the most powerful processes offered by Abraham (in my opinion). The basis of this process is the concept of appreciation. When you appreciate things and people around you, you feel better, because appreciation invokes the feeling of love.

I have heard Abraham differentiate between **"gratitude"** and **"appreciation"**. They say, and I interpret in my own words that an attitude of gratitude translates as "thank you for this, you gave it to me even though I was not deserving of it and therefore I am grateful". On the other hand, an attitude of appreciation is a more pure feeling place with none of the unworthiness that is contained in the word "gratitude". "I appreciate your giving me this", feels like a totally deserving perspective to hold and reflects more of an attitude of confident self- worth.

The more we appreciate the world around us and the things we see the more we express love and feel joy, the more time we spend in the Vortex.

Abraham says to get a special book and start writing in it all the things we appreciate about people in our lives.

Abraham suggests that we have a page in the book about each person or thing we wish to focus on. Abraham also suggests that we only write as much as flows easily – when coming up with things to write feels like too big an effort then it is time to stop.

"Every day make lists of positive aspects of the other and you and you will live happily ever after."
~ Abraham

I have noticed that as you write more and more, the process of writing gains momentum and so the more you have to appreciate, the more you have to appreciate. The more you have to fuss and worry about, the more you have to fuss and worry about.

Abraham has said on several occasions that the process of writing with an attitude of appreciation is more powerful than just thinking thoughts of appreciation or speaking thoughts of appreciation. The reason is that when we write out our thoughts we stay in the vibration of them longer than if we were only speaking them or feeling them. It is nice to spare fifteen minutes or so every day for this activity, and then you can add

thoughts of appreciation as you go about your day –
even lining up to get a coffee in the morning we can
appreciate how efficient the people are who are taking
orders and filling them.

When you start this work, it is better to start with things
that are easy to appreciate rather than try to find things
to appreciate about those aspects of your life that you
wish to improve. For example, if your objective is to
improve your relationship with money, it would be a
good idea to appreciate something or someone who has
nothing to do with the subject of money. This is because
you are Vibrationally too far away from the object of
your desire and attempting to jump up the emotional
scale doesn't usually work well (although it can), for
most people it works better to go up the scale in small
steps.

Abraham has also said that the feeling of appreciation or
joy is the same feeling place, whether you are looking at
and appreciating a flower or a child or a plate of your
favorite food. The feeling is the same, and it is the
feeling that is more important than the subject that
invokes the feeling, because the longer you stay in a
positive vibration the faster all things you want come
into your life. So the easiest thing to do is to appreciate
things or people in our lives that are easy to appreciate,

and not focus on anything or anyone that makes us feel unhappy.

"Appreciating is the thing. To be one who flows appreciation is really what you're after. To be one who gets appreciation is backwards, because it is almost always done from a lackful place."
~ Abraham

Focus Wheels

Focus wheeling is an exercise that Abraham teaches. The purpose of the exercise is to help raise vibration using general statements and then introduce the specific subject that you want to improve.

The analogy Abraham uses is that of getting on the merry-go-round in the park. If the merry-go-round is going very fast, and you want to get on it, you can't – the momentum prevents you from getting on. The only way you can get on is if you increase your speed to a level that you can jump on without being thrown off. So we increase our vibration using general statements and then when we are holding ourselves in a higher vibration with stability (stability is important – without it you will be thrown off the wheel).

Abraham recommends creating a circle with a smaller circle inside. The inner circle is a statement of the thing you wish to achieve – then you put twelve statements around the wheel of the things you want. And outside the circle you put a statement of the way things are that you wish to change. The objective is to form the statements in a manner that is one hundred percent reflective of the truth as well as one hundred percent true. Each successive statement increases the positive momentum of the thought process and this takes you closer to the end result you are seeking which is in the center of the wheel. This process keeps you in the vibration of the positive thoughts for over fifteen minutes and this is sufficient to activate a movement forward towards your chosen goal. Although you could think the statements out in your head or aloud, writing has more power because it takes longer to write a statement than to say it, and therefore, writing keeps you in the positive vibration longer and contributes more to the momentum of the positive stream of thought, creating a greater movement forward. Here is an example of a focus wheel.

There are no right or wrong statements – the only objective is to gather momentum on positive thoughts. The focus wheel takes practice but once you get the hang of it, it is one of the most powerful tools that you can use.

I personally find that when I do a list of positive aspects of the present situation, it gathers momentum and becomes a rampage of appreciation. As I continue with the momentum, the rampage then turns futuristic and the end result is a focus wheel. I do not draw a circle – I just write. It takes way more than just twelve statements for me to complete my exercise – but in the end it is very satisfying and I can actually feel movement on the subject – I can feel that my energy on the subject has shifted to a better place, because I feel better, and isn't that what it is all about?

"Don't talk yourself out of wanting something just because you haven't figured out how to get it."
~ Abraham

I feel fat

12. I like feeling good in my body

11. I am looking forward to making this change – it feels good, it feels right – I know I can do this

1. I have been slender before

10. I can get started right away with things I know and then more ideas will come – I am sure of it

2. I know that if others can do it then I can do it too

I want to be slender

9. It will feel good to be more flexible and agile

3. I just have to focus on finding something that works for me – there are so many options out there – I am sure there is one that works for me

8. It will be fun to buy new clothes

7. I already know some things that I can do that will help me achieve my goal

4. I know that once I put my mind to something I always find a way – I just have to be more open to ideas and I am willing to be open

6. I appreciate the strength and vitality of my physical body and the many functions it performs without my conscious involvement

5. I believe that my physical body responds to the way I think about it

103

If a tree falls in the forest...

More recently Abraham has been using the analogy of "a falling tree" in order to explain the process of translation or interpretation of energy by humans.

The point is, that if there is no translation or interpretation going on, then nothing is happening because there is no witness to it. So if a tree falls, and no one witnesses it then did the tree fall? If no one heard the noise of the tree falling, then was there any noise?

Our five physical senses are instruments with which we gather data from the world around us. This gathering of data is supposed to help us evaluate our preferences by considering the "contrasting information" and giving birth to desires. Once a desire is born then we must close the gap from the birthing of it to the receiving of it. So you see, everything starts with the translation of the vibration...everything starts when the tree falls in the forest and that vibration is translated by a receiver. That receiver could be human or animal or any point of consciousness. If there is no translation of energy then there is no creation of anything. It's the same principle as saying there are various radio stations transmitting all the time, but if I'm not tuning in to any of them, then for me none of them exist. If I was tuning in, then for me the only one that would exist would be the one that I was tuning into – and I would have to be on the same frequency as that particular station in order to receive a transmission from it.

"If a tree falls in a forest no one hears it - who cares, because if there is no receiver of the vibration of the sound then does it matter that there was a sound."
~ Abraham

The way to get rid of doubt

More recently this has become one of Abraham's favourite lines: "the way to get rid of doubt is before it starts".

The implicit meaning of this phrase is that we should have so much trust in the ability of the Universe to guide us to our greater well-being that whatever happens we never give in to negative emotion, we never doubt that things are working out for us. If we always live our life in alignment – giving birth to desires and lining up with them; if we never evaluate the pros and cons, and only look at the pros and appreciate the pros; if we appreciate where we are at all times, and love or life then there will never be any room for doubt and when there is no doubt in our vibration, there is no wobble, no resistance and all things that we want flow easily into our lives.

There never has to be any doubt to begin with, because everything is always alright. That's why the way to get rid of doubt is to prevent it from taking root – prevent that thought from ever gaining enough momentum that it has an impact on what manifests in your life. Abraham explains this with the analogy of the car on the top of a hill in San Francisco. If you put the car in neutral and nudged it forward it would start moving slowly, and when it first starts moving you can easily stop it by stepping in front of it and pushing it back, but if you wait too long and the car starts to move down the hill you can't step in front of it to stop it anymore because as it moves it gathers more and more speed or momentum, and if you tried to step in front of it, it would not end well for you.

"When you feel passion for something that makes you want to outwardly exude enthusiasm, in that moment of passion there is no doubt or negative expectation."
~ Abraham

Meditation

When you meditate you don't stop all thought – you just break your normal habit of thought for long enough for Source to take you to a better feeling place. As you keep reaching a better feeling place day after day after day – staying there becomes easier and easier and easier.

There is no right or wrong way to meditate. As Abraham says, "you cannot get it wrong" – it always helps. The first rule is: don't try to judge the quality of your meditation session. "Did I do it right? Did I get to the place of no thought?" There is no need for these questions, because all you are aiming for is to feel calmer. As with everything the more you practice the better you get, and so it is with meditation.

I use the Vortex Guided Meditation CD ever since it came out. I believe that the reading of the guide book that comes with the CD is as important as listening to the CD. You can use a guided meditation CD or just focus on your breathing.

Abraham recommends fifteen minutes of meditation everyday. They say that this is enough. I have on occasion done two sessions in a day – just when I want to stop and start my day again.

I like to pre-pave my meditation session with thoughts such as "I am going to meditate. I want to enjoy my meditation session and I want it to put me on a higher disc. I want my mediation to help me create more ease and flow in my life."

Meditation, as the word implies is not the absence of thought but a focused thought. The guided meditations help you focus on Abraham's words and Esther's voice and the music in the background – these act as anchors that enhance the meditation experience. However, you can meditate without these just as well. All you want to accomplish is to get away from your own thoughts. The dripping of a faucet, the hum of a machine, the process of breathing, repeating a phrase or a word are all meditative in nature, and they are all equally good techniques.

"Meditation is an effective tool because it quiets the mind and stops thought, so it stops resistant thought, therefore you're offering no resistance."
~ Abraham

Parting words

I believe that this book will continue to evolve in the same manner that Abraham is evolving their message to us. There will always be new analogies and new ways of looking at things, but the basic message has always been the same. From the beginning of time and through every Prophet in history, the message is the same – the only thing that changes is the interpretation we put on it. I have learnt much from Abraham and I continue to learn much – our paths continue to unfold.

There is great love here for you all.

Zehra
October 27, 2013
Revised April, 2015

"If you had only one goal, and that was to feel good, you would live successfully and happily, in a way of fulfilling your life's purpose, ever after."
~ Abraham

Appreciation

Much appreciation and love for Abraham, Esther and Jerry Hicks. Their dedication towards bringing the teachings to the world has changed many lives – mine included.

Much appreciation for Steve, because his asking inspired this little book through me. I have become the means through which the Universe has decided to being him the answers he is seeking – and I am having so much fun with this.

Much appreciation for my daughter Kinza, who has designed the perfect cover for this book.

I love my life and all those wonderful people who are co-creating with me.

Love & Blessings to All.

Zehra

www.zmahoon.com

About the Author

Zehra Mahoon lives in Ontario, Canada with her two beautiful children, Kinza and Faris, a hyper cat called Izzy and a lazy cat called Sitka. Zehra loves her home and her wooded backyard and the freedom she has in working from her home office. Over the past twelve years she has finally adjusted to the snow and cold weather in Ontario, but always welcomes a timely opportunity to get away to warmer places preferably with lots of old trees, rocks and water, good food and vibrant colours.

Zehra teaches weekly meditation classes at the local library. She loves to teach and write for her blog, as well as other journals and magazines. Zehra is an accomplished speaker and often makes television appearances. Aside from teaching the law of attraction, and offering financial advice , Zehra loves to cook and entertain and have fun with each new day of her life.

Zehra's other books include:

> The Prosperity Puzzle: your relationship with money and how to improve it

> Abraham 101: the basics of the law of attraction as taught by Abraham and understood by Me

If thoughts create then...how do people attract negative events they have never thought about? (free book available on Zehra's blog zmahoon.com)

Is this apple from my tree: a Law of Attraction Guide for parents and grandparents.

Zehra's books are available in digital and print formats through Amazon.com

Some of Zehra's popular blog posts based on the law of attraction, include:

Dream Big

Just say "Yes"

When people can't tell that they are being negative

How does it feel to win the lottery?

How beliefs are formed

For the love of food

Some Coaching Tips

Why does all hell break lose?

Can I get the man I want?

One Last Thing...

If you enjoyed this book or found it useful I would truly appreciate it if you would post a short review on Amazon. Your support really does make a difference and I read all the reviews personally so I can get your feedback and make this book even better.

Much love and appreciation,

Zehra

26094960R00070

Made in the USA
San Bernardino, CA
19 November 2015